BOOKS IN THE MERCIFULLY BRIEF, REAL WORLD SERIES

Raising Thousands (if Not Tens of Thousands) of Dollars with Email
by Madeline Stanionis • Emerson & Church, Publishers • $24.95

After reading the title of this book perhaps you're saying, "Sure, Red Cross and UNICEF can raise tons of money with email, but my agency isn't a brand name. You're telling me I can do the same!?"

Well, no. Author Madeline Stanionis is President of Donordigital, not Pollyanna. But what she is saying is that you can have surprising success if you approach email fundraising with a measure of intelligence and creativity.

Generously dispensing advice and insider tips, Stanionis reveals precisely what you need to do, step by step, to raise substantial money with email.

Raising More Money with Newsletters than You Ever Thought Possible
by Tom Ahern • Emerson & Church, Publishers • $24.95

Today, countless organizations are raising more money with their newsletter than with traditional mail appeals. And after reading Tom Ahern's riveting book, it's easy to understand why.

For starters, the newsletters Ahern shows you how to write deliver real news, not tired features. They make the donor feel important. They use emotional triggers to spur action. They're designed in a way to attract both browsers and readers. And they don't depend on dry statistics to make the organization's case.

Transforming your newsletter into a powerful money raiser isn't all that difficult ... assuming you follow Ahern's perceptive advice.

Raising $1,000 Gifts by Mail
by Mal Warwick • Emerson & Church, Publishers • $24.95

Whoever heard of raising $1,000 gifts (not to mention $3,000, $4,000 and $5,000 gifts) by mail? That's the province of personal solicitation, right? Not exclusively, says Mal Warwick.

With carefully selected examples and illustrations, Warwick shows you how to succeed with high-dollar mail, walking you step by step through the process of identifying your prospects, crafting the right letter, the right brochure, the right response device, and the right envelope.

Attracting the Attention Your Cause Deserves
by Joseph Barbato • Emerson & Church, Publishers • $24.95

Think of Attracing the Attention Your Cause Deserves as a "Trade Secrets Revealed" book, one allowing you to accomplish three key objectives for your cause: greater visibility, a broader constituency, and more money raised.

With more than a million nonprofit organizations in existence, there's a lot of noise out there. Shouting won't get you noticed - everyone's doing that. And everybody's tuning it out.

What will attract attention is following the field-tested advice that spills over every single page of this illuminating book.

Raising Money
Through Bequests

How Your Organization Can Profit
From the Biggest Intergenerational Transfer
of Wealth in History

Emerson & Church
Real World Guides

First printed April 2007

10 9 8 7 6 5 4 3 2 1

Printed in the United States of America

This text is printed on acid-free paper.

Copies of this book are available from the publisher at discount when purchased in quantity.

Emerson & Church, Publishers
P.O. Box 338, Medfield, MA 02052
Tel. 508-359-0019
Fax 508-359-2703
www.emersonandchurch.com

Library of Congress Cataloging-in-Publication Data

Valinsky, David.
  Raising money through bequests : how your organization can profit from the biggest intergenerational transfer of wealth in history
 / David Valinsky and Melanie Boyd.
     p. cm.
  ISBN-13: 978-1-889102-29-0 (pbk. : alk. paper)
  1. Charitable bequests. I. Boyd, Melanie. II. Title.
  HV25.V35 2007
  658.15'224—dc22

2007000711

Raising Money Through Bequests

How Your Organization Can Benefit
From the Biggest Intergenerational Transfer
of Wealth in History

DAVID VALINSKY & MELANIE BOYD

Emerson
& Church
PUBLISHERS

To my wife Lorrie and daughter Alex

– David Valinsky

In memory of my parents, Evelyn and Bill,
who taught me the importance of giving

– Melanie Boyd

A Talmudic story tells of a traveler who once saw a man planting a carob tree. He asked him when he thought the tree would bear fruit.

"After seventy years" was the reply.

"Dost thou expect to live seventy years and eat the fruit of thy labor?"

"I did not find the world desolate when I entered it," said the old man, "and as my ancestors planted for me before I was born, so do I plant for those who will come after me."

CONTENTS

DONOR FOLLOW UP

FINAL THOUGHTS

APPENDIX

1

It's Easier than You Think

You've just completed a successful annual appeal, you've done your share of special events, and you've properly recognized and thanked the top donors to your organization.

Everything's going great.

Then, at the next board meeting, one of your volunteers (perhaps based on her experience with another group) asks the question, "What are we doing about bequests and planned giving?"

If the answer is "Nothing" or "Not much," you're not alone. The truth is, a large number of organizations haven't begun to address planned giving or are in the early stages of setting up a program.

If this describes you, then bequests are the easiest and most logical place to start.

As you'll learn in the following pages, there are a host of simple and concrete steps you can take right now to greatly increase your chances of receiving bequests.

Sometimes they'll be small – 10 shares of GE perhaps. But if you plan and implement your program properly, there'll come a day when you open the mail and learn that you're the recipient of a sizable, perhaps transformative, bequest.

John Kennedy loved to tell the story of the great French Marshal Lyautey, who once asked his gardener to plant a tree. The gardener objected that the tree was slow-growing and wouldn't mature for a hundred years. The Marshal replied, "In that case, there is no time to lose, plant it this afternoon."

Good advice with bequests. Let's get started now.

2

Are You Ready to Launch A Bequest Program?

We know what you're thinking.

You want to know if your organization, which isn't a brand name, can raise money through bequests.

Here's the answer and we think you'll be pleased with it.

You can, and it'll be easier than you think, provided you can answer "Yes" to the following:

• Is your organization a 501(c)3 nonprofit tax exempt organization? Donors will often ask to make sure, and won't give to you if you aren't.

• Is your organization mission-driven? Do all of your programs and services meet the mission and is that mission known in the community?

• Are you established in the community? How long has your organization been in existence? Donors want assurance that the organizations they support will still be there tomorrow.

• Do you have a recognized track record of success? In other words, are you not only succeeding in meeting your mission, but also sharing the good news? If not, you may want to focus your efforts here first.

• Do you have the necessary staff and volunteer support? Initially, the responsibility for your bequest program may be tacked on to the duties of an existing staff member. But as your program grows, a new staff person may be required.

• Do you have an existing donor base? Have you conducted an annual appeal? Was it successful? Donors rarely make their first gift to an organization in the form of a bequest; typically, they will have already supported your organization in other ways first.

• Do you communicate with your donors on a regular basis? How often do you thank and recognize your current donors? When is the last time you visited a donor at her home or invited her to take a private tour of your organization?

• Is your organizational leadership well respected? If you've just made a big change in leadership or their ability has been questioned, it's probably better to focus on public relations first.

• Is your organization perceived as stable? Change is inevitable. But, if you've just come under 'new management' or were the recent focus of a nasty public relations snafu, now isn't the time to launch a bequest program.

3

Now's The Time

Often, when we first meet with the staff and volunteer leadership of an organization to discuss planned giving, we start by sharing some big numbers:

$260.30 billion

$199.07 billion

$ 17.44 billion

$260.30 billion: That's the amount U.S. donors gave in 2005. Of that, $199.07 billion came from living individuals (not foundations, not corporations). Most importantly for our purposes here, *$17.44 billion was given through bequests, representing 7 percent of total estimated giving.*

And the sum is likely to grow, as we're in the middle of a transfer of wealth unlike any we've experienced before.

■ The Greatest Generation

Not long ago, A. Charles Schultz published an article entitled *Four*

Golden Years. The title refers to the years between 2004 and 2007 when members of "The Greatest Generation" are in their 80s and 90s, many with sizable assets to bequeath. He describes three personal characteristics of this proud population.

They're optimistic. Having survived the Great Depression, they know they can surmount just about any obstacle.

They're civic-minded. Having helped to rebuild economies and nations in the wake of World War II, as well as shape labor unions and enact legislation for the common good, they take their role as citizens seriously. They also understand the key role of philanthropy.

They're careful accumulators. The Great Depression saw an unprecedented 25 percent unemployment rate, teaching a difficult lesson of the importance of saving and investing.

Owing largely to this last characteristic, many of these "Depression babies" won't make large gifts during their lifetime. The majority of their six- and seven-figure gifts will come through planned gifts, including bequests.

This unprecedented transfer of wealth will affect charitable organizations now and for years to come. Together these two groups, the Greatest Generation and their Baby Boomer children, will pass on some $14 trillion by 2052. A sizable portion of it will go to charitable organizations (hopefully one of them will be yours).

4

Making Dreams Come True: The Real Reasons Donors Make Bequests

We've led off many a meeting and workshop with the following question: "What do you think are the top five reasons donors give to charitable organizations?"

Invariably, "tax purposes" is mentioned, often cited as key. But in reality the motivations for philanthropy run much deeper, and IRS concerns may not even figure in the top ten.

From our conversations with donors, here are the most common reasons they give to philanthropic causes.

1) They believe in the mission.

This is the number one reason why people give, and we find it holds true for bequest giving as well. Donors are inspired by the mission of the organization and its commitment to changing or saving lives in the community.

2) They've seen the mission realized firsthand.

One way donors can confirm the value of their giving is through firsthand experience. Maybe they've worked for your organization as volunteers. Perhaps they serve on the board and recently attended a meeting where a social worker talked about the difference your food bank is making in one family's life. Or it could be they attended a special event where an alumnus spoke eloquently about the education he received at your university.

3) They know you'll use their gift wisely.

Donors want their gifts stewarded and carefully spent. (It's pretty much the same with tax dollars. We get angry, for instance, at the Pentagon squandering $600 for a simple hammer.) Organizations that are mindful of their disbursements and regularly report to donors on how their gift has changed the lives of others set the stage for bequest giving.

4) Your organization has directly impacted their life or the life of a loved one.

"You have cancer." Those were the first three words of a brochure we wrote for a cancer center campaign. This simple phrase forged an immediate connection between the prospective donor and the cancer center's mission. Who among us haven't heard these words in connection with a family member, friend, or co-worker. Few of us know just how many lives are touched by the organizations we serve. But those to whom we've really mattered won't soon forget us.

5) They feel like they know you.

At heart, successful fundraising is about building relationships. About staying in touch with donors, whether by phone, personal visit, email, or birthday card. That's why, despite your pressing meeting with the invitation designer or that grant report due next week, making the time to reach out to your donors must always be the first order of business.

6) It feels good to give.

As good as it feels to receive a special gift, those of us who are philanthropic also know how good it feels to give. Jerold Panas, author of *Mega Gifts* and other classic books on fundraising, talks about "enlightened-givers" – generous women and men who love to give. "For enlightened-givers, there's a sense that they're only trustees of the money they've earned or inherited. They find it wonderful fun to give money to help those in need. They find making a gift to be a rollicking experience."

7) They hold the staff and volunteer leadership in high regard.

For donors, the face of your organization is often the person whose name is at the top of the organizational chart or a staff or board member who has had direct contact with them. How this individual is perceived – most notably, their unquestioned integrity – is often what dictates whether a donor will give a consequential gift.

8) They appreciate and benefit from your organization's products and services.

An enjoyable night at the theatre. A challenging Pilates class. A particularly moving Mass during the holidays. The attentiveness of a healthcare professional during a serious illness. Any of these may be incentive enough for an individual to take the next step and make a gift.

9) It allows them to honor or memorialize a loved one.

What we find in many situations is that people want to leave a lasting memorial to their loved one, especially when that loved one had a connection to your organization. A memorial gift provides a way to keep their memory – and spirit – alive.

10) It serves the need to be accepted and to belong.

While recognition isn't important to everyone, many of us want to be part of a special group. Families and friends meet this need for many. But so do charitable organizations. That in part explains why just over 50 percent of all 2005 contributions went to two types of organizations – education and religion – both of which forge strong feelings of belonging.

5

Getting Started

To get your program started, you'll need to follow a few simple steps:

• Familiarize yourself with the basic terms and types of bequest giving.

• Understand the benefits of having an up-to-date will and why many people don't.

• Become acquainted with the various benefits your donor will be entitled to when making a bequest.

This easy to grasp background will provide the comfort level you need to carry on a simple conversation with your donor. It isn't necessary to discuss every detail and technical aspect of a will – often that will be for your donors' professional advisor to explain. Instead, your goal is to offer some basic information and – most importantly – to explain how your donor's support is instrumental in achieving the outcomes you both want.

■ Getting Your Terms Straight

All professions have their jargon – helpful to those 'in the know' but confusing to those on the outside. Although many of us understand the basic vocabulary of fundraising, few are comfortable using the language of bequests and estate planning.

Our hope here is to demystify the technical jargon to allow you to speak in clear and simple terms with your donors.

Let's start with the will.

• The Will

In its simplest terms, a will is a document used to distribute assets. It allows donors to leave certain portions of their estate to individuals and causes they care about. Each state establishes specific requirements (statutes) for a valid will, and it's important to encourage donors to consult with an attorney to draft this document.

Keep these startling statistics in mind: *Only 40 percent of all adults and only 70 percent of adults over the age of 55 have wills.* And if there's no will, there's zero possibility your organization will receive a bequest. Your number one priority, throughout the life of your bequest program, is educating your donors on the importance of creating a will.

• Why Do You Need a Will?

This simplest of documents is important for a number of reasons:

• By means of a will, you can establish trusts to invest and manage assets for your beneficiaries (a college fund for grandchildren, for instance).

• You can provide specific bequests to loved ones (think of a cherished heirloom that's been in your family for years).

• A will can help save taxes and avoid unnecessary expenses on the administration of your estate.

• And, of course, a will allows you to make charitable bequests to your favorite causes.

• What are the Consequences of Not Having a Will?

Creating a will allows donors to distribute their assets as they see fit; not having a will places that control elsewhere.

• An executor – possibly a stranger – can be nominated to handle your estate.

• You may lose the option of nominating who you want to serve as the guardian for any children considered minors.

• Without a will ("dying intestate"), the state determines how your property is divided up.

• Why People Don't Have Wills

Certainly, there are personal reasons people put off drawing up a will. They may be uncomfortable contemplating their own death or deciding who will get what. Then, too, a number of misconceptions keep individuals from creating a will.

• *My spouse will automatically get everything.* Not true, and under most state laws, the children may share in the distribution of assets.

• *Everything is jointly held.* While many people assume that property will always pass to the surviving spouse, this isn't always the case. For example, a collection of valuable jewelry may be required to be divided between a spouse and the children based upon state statutes. And what if both spouses die together in an accident?

• *I'm single.* Certainly this is no reason to leave the distribution of your assets up to your state of residence.

• *I don't have enough assets.* Perhaps. But you still want the assets you do have distributed in accordance with your wishes.

• Charitable Bequests

A charitable bequest is a written statement in your will directing that a gift be made to a certain charity (the beneficiary) upon the death of the person establishing the will. Often, a donor will bequeath a parcel of real estate, a sum of money, a specific amount of stock, or even a home. Upon the individual's death, the bequest is said to have "matured."

Note: Of those individuals who make charitable bequests, one-third provide for more than one charity, with the average donor giving to five or six organizations. In addition, only about 11 percent of donors change the terms of their bequests, and fewer than 9 percent have ever removed a charity from their will. So, while bequests are certainly revocable by law, they appear to be much less so in actual practice.

- **Types of Bequests**

  GENERAL BEQUEST - A specific dollar amount or a specific asset

  I leave $100,000 to ABC Charity.
  I leave my summer home to ABC Charity.

  PERCENTAGE BEQUEST - A percentage of the total estate

  I give ABC charity property equal to 20% of my total estate.

  RESIDUARY BEQUEST - A percentage of, or entire, residue

  After distribution of specific items, I leave 40% of the remainder of my estate to ABC Charity.

  After all of my debts, expenses, and bequests are distributed, I leave the remainder to ABC Charity.

  CONTINGENT BEQUEST - Result of a certain condition being met

  In the event that my wife does not survive me, I leave the property set aside for her to ABC Charity.

In addition, charitable bequests may be designated as unrestricted or restricted to benefit a certain program. Donors may also specify that their bequests be used to create or expand an endowment fund where only the income from the fund is used and the principal remains intact, or to allow for their annual support to continue in perpetuity.

6

Gain Board Approval

A new bequest program typically requires formal support from the board of directors. But for the program to be successful, you'll also need the active participation of individual board members. A presentation to the board can help you achieve both.

If you're fortunate, a committed board member will introduce the concept and advocate for the program. But it may also fall on the shoulders of staff to encourage board approval.

Regardless of who spearheads the presentation, you'll want to include the following elements:

1) Give a brief report on the history of bequests your organization has received

> *How many unsolicited bequests have we received?*
> *When were they received?*
> *Who were the donors?*
> *What was their connection to the organization?*

2) Explain how a bequest program will help benefit donors and friends

As we've said, a bequest program offers you the opportunity to educate people on the importance of having a will. This in itself is a worthy service to your constituents. But, as important, through your bequest program you're offering individuals the very real opportunity of making a dramatic and lasting impact on the community.

3) Review the benefits to the organization, as well as the cost to introduce and operate the program

Unlike special events and annual appeals, revenue from a bequest program can take years to realize. And that's the sticking point for many board members ("We can't afford this right now," they'll argue). Counter this response by asking a simple question: where would your organization be today if years ago its leadership had worked toward ensuring a steady stream of bequests? It's up to the current board to ensure that future generations will have the benefit of their visionary planning.

4) Suggest personnel to staff the program

All organizations are staffed differently. Initially, responsibility for your bequest program will fall to the development director, marketing or public relations director or, in very small organizations, to the executive director. Therefore, in the early stages, you may not incur additional staff expenses, although there will be expenses related to programming and materials. Still, make it clear to the board that as the program matures and gift revenue increases, additional staffing may be required.

5) Address common myths of donor bequest decision making

As part of your board presentation, it can be eye-opening to address several prevailing myths.

- *Donors' estate plans are mostly driven by tax considerations*

Although estate tax reductions based on charitable giving are important to donors, they rank lower in priority than you would think. Noted planned giving author Kathryn W. Mire, JD contends that tax incentives are rarely the primary motivation for a gift, and we agree.

Rather, the decision to do something special for an organization is motivated by the donor's belief in its mission. The thought process typically starts with: "I want to do something for my church." It's at that moment that the decision is made. Tax benefits are a secondary reward the donor is happy to accept, but by no means the driving force.

- *Donors want to leave their entire estate to their children*

When we introduce this particular myth, most heads nod. But when we query people further, we usually hear the following responses:

I want to take care of college and provide something substantial, but my children don't need it all.

My children are doing great; I don't need to give them everything.

I "made it" on my own and I want my kids to make it on their own too.

To be sure, spouses, kids, grandchildren, nieces and nephews influence our decision, but the wish to "leave it all to the children" – while it sometimes may be what our donors want – should never be assumed.

Ideally, what you want from this presentation to the board is their formal approval and adoption of the program. But, at the very least, if objection after objection is raised, work toward some general consensus that the program merits further review. Then, behind the scenes, with key individuals whose support you do have, outline your follow-up strategy to help the board as a whole understand the importance of implementing a bequest program.

7

Forming a Bequest Advisory Committee

Although some Bequest Advisory Committees are composed solely of professional advisors (e.g. lawyers, trust officers, investment managers, insurance agents and financial planners), a mix of volunteers and board members – regardless of their profession – is ideal.

We form our opinions through experience. Thus, while a lawyer may look at bequests from one angle, a doctor whose patient made a bequest after her life was saved may hold another. The diversity of opinion will typically strengthen your committee.

As for recruiting committee members, well, that's never easy as we're sure you know. But your best candidates are likely to be volunteers with a real passion for your cause. Often, they may have already established a bequest or another planned gift arrangement. If they haven't, more than likely they will as the process develops.

■ Responsibilities

Whether your initial committee includes a mere handful of people or a dedicated team of 10 or more, their duties will usually include the following:

1) Attend Bequest Advisory Committee meetings and actively participate in the program.

2) Assist in the creation of the bequest society (develop a format, establish membership eligibility and appropriate recognition, and create initial marketing plans).

3) Review and recommend gift acceptance policies.

4) Assist staff in implementing and marketing the program.

5) Serve as ambassadors and advocates to the board and in the community. This includes a willingness to speak to different groups and selected individuals about the bequest program.

6) Identify prospects and when appropriate accompany staff on personal visits.

7) Become a member of the bequest society.

This last point is particularly important. To be successful, your bequest program must start with your inner family. Advisory committee members, board members and staff too – each of these groups should be among the first to be educated about, and invited to join, your bequest society.

While not all staff and board members will do so, based on their commitment to your organization, all members of your advisory committee should also be members of your bequest society. And the earlier they do so, the better advocates they will become.

8

Your First Bequest Advisory Committee Meeting

For the first meeting of your Bequest Advisory Committee, you'll need a well thought-out agenda that includes generous time at the end for questions.

It also helps, prior to the meeting, to designate a chair or coordinator for the committee.

Sample Agenda

I. *Welcome*

- The lead staff member or committee coordinator provides a warm welcome, and thanks everyone for agreeing to participate.

- If the head of the organization can attend, he or she also expresses gratitude and stresses how the committee will benefit the organization today and in the future.

II. *Introduction*

- Those in attendance introduce themselves and share their feelings about the organization. Ask the committee coordinator to begin the process by describing why he or she is involved. While this portion of the agenda may take some time, it's important for a number of reasons:

   A. Sharing their own stories will remind attendees of how deeply they care about your organization's mission.
   B. They'll start to bond as a group, even if they already know one another.
   C. You just might identify some eloquent spokespersons for your program.
   D. One or more of those present may have a compelling story you can use in your case for support or future articles.
   E. And, some may even inform you that they've already made a bequest to the organization.

   We've used this exercise with all types of volunteer fundraising groups, and inevitably both staff and volunteers are inspired by the process.

III. *Provide an orientation to bequests*

- Use the Bequest Test (in the Appendix) to start the committee thinking about bequest giving and what it could mean for your organization.
- Give a short overview of bequests (much of which can come from your presentation to the board: see Chapter Six).

   - Definition of terms
   - Types of bequests

- Common misconceptions

IV. *Explain what you're hoping to accomplish*

   A. To generate funding for the organization by tapping into the tremendous potential represented by bequests.
   B. To educate people about bequests and the need for a current will.
   C. To provide yet another opportunity for people to connect with and support the organization.

V. *Begin a discussion of possible benefits for members of the Bequest Society:*

- We'll talk more about incentives for donors in a later chapter.

VI. *The role of the bequest advisory committee*

- Review the purpose of the Bequest Advisory Committee and the role of its members (see previous chapter).

VII. *Identify possible themes of the case for support*

- Through a group discussion, begin to identify key themes for the case for support. The final case may be four paragraphs or four pages long! Regardless, you'll want the committee's input. (We'll talk more about this key document in the next chapter.)

VIII. *Discussion of next steps*

- Determine who will be responsible for completing the necessary projects prior to the next meeting.

- Create a first draft of the case for support based on committee input.
- Identify people who are prospects for bequests.
- Produce an initial draft of gift acceptance policies (more on these in a later chapter).
- Create bequest society membership requirements.

IX. *Set next meeting and adjourn*

- You'll want to hold your second meeting four to six weeks after the first. You'll have a lot to cover, of course, but be certain that a good working draft of your case for support is sent to committee members prior to the meeting.

9

Crafting a Vision of Tomorrow: The Case for Support

Immediately after the first meeting of your Bequest Advisory Committee, a preliminary case for support should be drafted.

Traditionally used in capital campaigns, a case for support (often called a case statement) tells the story of your organization and engages the reader with your vision for the future. Successful cases appeal to the head *and* the heart. They use a blend of hard data and heart-tugging.

If, for example, yours is a group serving the elderly, you might emphasize how your transportation services provide daily trips for 150 people to the local hospital or supermarket (the 'head' numbers), allowing them the dignity of remaining independent in their later years (the 'heart' appeal). If yours is a symphony, you could describe how your programs for 2,000 children in area schools nurture their love for music while also enriching lives through the artistry of music. Whatever benefits you focus on, don't hesitate to look twenty, fifty, or even one-hundred years into the future.

■ Case Components

When developing your case, you'll need to answer two questions:

1) Why do the people we serve need the donor's support?
2) How will the donor's bequest help change or save lives?

On the next page is a portion of the case for St. Anthony Medical Center (in the Appendix, you'll find a complete sample case). Here's why we think the St. Anthony piece is effective:

1) The case is connected to the organization's mission early on.
2) Statistics are used throughout to appeal to the reader's rational side.
3) The use of a question – "Who, then, will see to the needs?" – indirectly asks the reader to consider their own support.
4) Words like "devastating" and "disturbing" seek to draw the reader in emotionally.
5) The organization is presented as the answer to the problems cited.
6) The invitation to support the organization is set up early (and stated outright in a later section).

Excerpt from the case statement of St. Anthony Medical Center

WHAT DOES THE FUTURE HOLD?

1 The health care institutions of the Franciscan Sisters of the Poor exist to serve people, not to make a profit. Monies earned by these hospitals are put back into those institutions to enhance their work. Each facility desperately needs privately-raised funds to sustain the Mission into the next century.

Futurists tell us that health care will continue to be an expensive business. The costs of machinery and manpower will continue to rise. Patients admitted to hospitals in the future will be sicker and require more extensive care than patients of the past.

Many of these patients will be elderly. **2**

By the year 2000, 4.9 million Americans will be over age 85. Fifty percent of all health care expenses will be related to caring for those age 65 or older.

By the early part of the 21st century, one in five Americans will be over the age of 65. A large portion of these people will have Alzheimer's disease and other debilitating illnesses. Because many of these Baby Boomers did not marry or have children, they will be forced to look outside the family for long term caretaking. Even more disturbing, this generation may lack financial reserves to pay for that care.

3 WHO, THEN, WILL SEE TO THE NEEDS OF THESE PEOPLE? **4**

If being elderly in the 21st century will be a problem, being poor will be devastating. We know that American society is becoming polarized with the rich growing richer, the poor growing poorer, and the middle class quietly disappearing.

Even today, many of the poor who need health care cannot afford to pay for it. Only about 40% of Americans living below the poverty line are covered by Medicaid. In 1989, Ohio hospitals provided about $405.5 million in care to persons who could not or did not pay their bills. Currently, one in seven Ohioans has no health insurance nor any way to pay for medical care. Thirty percent of these medically indigent persons are under age 18 with little hope of changing their lifestyles as they grow older. Across the country, 37 million Americans are uninsured and millions more are underinsured.

By the 21st century, the role for the federal government in providing health care for the less fortunate will be even further diminished. Many of the poor will be full-time workers, employed by companies who either cannot or will not provide health insurance as a benefit.

WHO WILL SEE TO THE NEEDS OF THESE PEOPLE?

Public opinion polls show that nearly 70 percent of all Americans feel that government should be responsible for providing health care for the poor. But those same polls also show that in difficult economic times, tax funding for that health care becomes a low priority to most citizens. **5**

SO, WHO WILL SEE TO THE NEEDS OF THESE PEOPLE?

Institutions like Saint Anthony Medical Center are more than willing to bear the burden. But, they cannot do it without your help. **6**

10

Gift Acceptance Policies

A brief set of gift acceptance policies is essential if you're undertaking a bequest program.

The good news is that most bequests will be rather simple and easy to accept. Typically, you'll learn of them through a letter from the donor's attorney.

But there will be some bequests that present problems, and here's where gift acceptance policies come in handy.

Clear policies set guidelines for what types of gifts you'll accept. For our purposes, these will be bequests of cash, securities, real estate, and properties (e.g. jewelry, art, vehicles) of any description.

What if a donor has bequeathed a high-mileage, run-down pickup? What if an intended gift of real estate has environmental problems? What if securities left to you are in a company that subverts your mission (e.g. tobacco funding for a cancer fighting organization)?

It's important to address these kinds of issues so that your board can comfortably disclaim a bequest that may create legal or administrative problems.

■ Sample Gift Acceptance Policy Language

A. *The Bequest*

1) Cash, securities, real estate, or property of any description may be bequeathed to THE ORGANIZATION by a clause in the donor's Will or by a Codicil added to the Will. The donor using this method retains full control and use of the property during his lifetime and may alter or revoke the bequest at any time.

2) At the time of the donor's death, the bequest qualifies as a charitable deduction for estate tax purposes. The bequest does not, however, provide the donor with any tax advantages during her lifetime, nor does it provide an assured income for donors or their beneficiaries, as other plans may.

B. *Acceptance and Approval of Planned and Deferred Gifts*

1) In every instance, official acceptance of all planned and deferred gifts will be made by the board of directors, based upon the recommendation of the president. Only those gifts which are in conformity with the needs of THE ORGANIZATION will be accepted. [This language is typically included to protect against a restricted bequest that funds a program which no longer exists, wants to introduce a new program which doesn't match the organization's mission, or presents a risk to the organization]

2) THE ORGANIZATION reserves the right to refuse any gift, which is judged to be inconsistent with THE ORGANIZATION'S needs or for which THE ORGANIZATION'S resources are too limited to properly administer. In addition, only those gifts from which disbursements are to be made on a nondiscriminatory basis in conformance with affirmative action programs and policies are to be accepted.

11

Setting Up
A Bequest Society

More and more organizations are using bequest societies to promote their bequest programs.

In essence, a bequest society is simply a way to encourage and thank donors for their willingness to support your organization by establishing a bequest.

It's also the principal marketing tool for your program.

■ Creating a Name

Typical names for bequest societies include *The Heritage Society, The Legacy Society,* or even, more simply, *The Bequest Society.* (Additional names appear in the Appendix.) Any of these are fine. However, you may want a name that accentuates your organization's history or even a past bequest donor. For example:

The 1914 Society: The organization's incorporation date

The Broad Street Society: Location of the facility
The William Jones Society: Founder of the organization

■ Membership Requirements

In addition to an appealing name, you'll also want to establish eligibility requirements. Here, the most important consideration is this: *make it as easy as possible for the donor to join your society.* Some organizations simply ask donors to inform them of their intent. Others require that a form be filled out and signed.

■ Membership Recognition and Benefits

Once you've identified a bequest donor, the head of the organization should send a thank you letter acknowledging the individual as a new member of your bequest society. The coordinator of your advisory committee might also send a second thank you letter, inviting the new member to contact her with any questions.

As to the benefits for the donor, these might include any of the following:
- A society certificate or pin
- A newsletter that includes topical articles on estate planning
- An invitation to an annual luncheon
- Permanent recognition on a wall display

We know of one performing arts organization that literally places donors 'center stage'. The night before the performance, they host a recognition luncheon on the stage itself.

Regardless of how you recognize your donors, what matters most is that you do recognize them and do so often.

12

The Bequest Society Brochure

A well-done brochure introducing your bequest society will often serve as your best means of communication with prospects. The brochure should include your case for support (or an abridged version of it); some brief, interesting history of your organization; and a return card allowing donors to request more information or notify you of their intent to leave a bequest.

Make sure your inaugural publication has a shelf life of one to two years since you'll often want to use it as a "leave-behind" piece for visits with potential donors.

■ Components of a Bequest Society Brochure

In your brochure, you'll want to include the following:

1. Your bequest society's name
2. How to make a bequest to your organization
3. Who to contact for more information
4. A way for the reader to respond (postcard, self-addressed envelope)

5. An invitation to join the society (sometimes this is forgotten!)

You may also want to include a brief letter from your president or executive director introducing the brochure and the new program.

Your brochure needn't be as elaborate as the sample that follows, provided it includes the five key components we cited above.

Here are some of the reasons that the brochure works well, in our opinion (see corresponding numbers on facing page):

1) The Sister depicted on the cover is a much beloved and respected leader of the organization.
2) The title of the lead article is an invitation to join. From the very beginning, the reader is engaged.
3) The invitation to join is repeated at the bottom and set off visually.
4) There is clear contact information on the front.
5) Emotional appeals and touching stories personalize the organization for the reader.
6) Clear methods of giving are explained for the reader.
7) A pledge form is enclosed, allowing the donor to inform Mother Cabrini of their gift or to request additional information.
8) The benefits of membership are listed.

Cabrini Connections Newsletter

MOTHER CABRINI LEGACY SOCIETY NEWSLETTER

GOLDEN, COLORADO

VOLUME 1 , 2001

Cabrini CONNECTIONS

HEALING, TEACHING, CARING, GIVING

Will You Walk This Road With Us?

Sr. Bernadette Casciano, MSC, Administrator of Mother Cabrini Shrine.

FOR MORE INFORMATION, CONTACT:

Mother Cabrini Shrine
Sr. Bernadette Casciano, MSC,
Administrator

JoAnn Seaman,
Director of Development

Phone: 303.526.0758

Visit us on the web:
www.den-cabrini-shrine.org
www.mothercabrini.com
www.cabrinifoundation.org

by Sr. Bernadette Casciano, MSC

Holy ground. When visitors experience the sacred space so much loved by St. Frances Cabrini at the top of her mountain in Golden, Colorado, they can't help but exclaim that they have walked on holy ground - and they have. We are blessed to be able to walk the path Mother Cabrini, her Sisters and the children took through the hills and to the top of the mountain to rest, to pray and to come closer to the Heart of Christ.

Continue the journey. You are invited to walk with the Cabrinian family on a pilgrimage of faith to journey to the top of the mountain, to find your sacred space, to recognize the role you play in continuing the legacy of Mother Cabrini... to *"Bring the love of Christ to the world!"*

The Mother Cabrini Legacy Society has been created to unite the Cabrinian family together to accept Mother Cabrini's challenge to "help the missions entrusted to the Institute of the Missionary Sisters of the Sacred Heart by offerings and service." **How?** The Society specifically focuses on charitable and estate planning and the structuring of bequests and planned gift options. **Why?** For some, these gifts express gratitude for blessings received... for others, thanksgiving for the caring compassionate presence and services of Cabrini sisters, institutions, programs and ministries... and for all who want to give back, to do more, to make a difference.

The Stairway to Prayer leads to the top of the mountain, where the statue of the Sacred Heart resides, at Mother Cabrini Shrine in Golden, Colorado.

Please join us in sustaining this Cabrini legacy and heritage of mission — walking together in faith, love and the desire to create a better world for today and future generations.

Cabrini Connections Newsletter: Page 1

Cabrini Connections Newsletter (continued)

Page 2  Mother Cabrini Legacy Society 2001

The Legacy of Mother Cabrini

⑤ Frances Cabrini was an ordinary, fragile woman who was transformed by a powerful, personal experience of God's love. She walked and worked on the streets and in the cities of this country carrying this love of God to people in need — especially the immigrants looking to make a new and better life. Through hard work and simple direct service, she founded schools, orphanages and hospitals where she went about her everyday task of healing, teaching, caring and giving to those who needed her love, help and attention.

Her legacy lives today on five continents and cities all over the world. The Missionary Sisters of the Sacred Heart of Jesus and all people of faith who follow Mother Cabrini's example seek to respond to her words:

Can we not multiply the joys of the heart of Jesus by our prayers, works and winning over of hearts and souls who will love him even more? Let us imitate the charity of his Heart and make ourselves all things to all people to win them all to Jesus.

Ways to Give... Ways to Give... Ways to Give

⑥ There are a number of planned (deferred) giving options, regardless of size, available to you as you consider joining our Mother Cabrini Legacy Society. These gifts, through the Society, will serve to support the future needs and programs of the Shrine.

PLANNED GIFTS

Bequests

Gifts by will may be for a specific dollar amount, a percentage of the total estate or the residuum remaining after all debts, taxes, expenses and other bequests have been paid. Specific bequests of property such as real estate may also be made.

Gift Annuities

In exchange for a gift of cash or securities the Cabrini Fund, Inc. will guarantee to pay you and/or another beneficiary a specified annuity. This is one of the oldest and simplest ways of making a gift and in addition to the current charitable deduction a portion of each annuity payment is income tax free.

Tax Deferred Retirement Plan

What has become very popular in recent years is naming a charity as a beneficiary in ones tax deferred retirement plan such as an IRA, Keough Plans, 401(k) plans and 403(b) plans. The distribution from any of these plans would take place after your death and may be very tax-wise for your family.

Life Insurance

Policies that are no longer needed for family protection or business purposes make excellent charitable gifts, regardless of whether or not all of the premiums have been paid. When ownership of the policy is irrevocably assigned to Mother Cabrini Shrine, the cash value of the policy is a tax deductible gift, as are all future premium payments. By establishing new life insurance policies, specifically for Mother Cabrini Shrine, a donor is able to make a substantial gift for a relatively modest annual outlay.

Life Income Gifts

Charitable remainder unitrusts or annuity trusts enable you to make a significant gift to the Shrine while protecting or greatly improving your person financial position. You and/or another named beneficiary will receive the income from the trust for your lives and you also receive an immediate income tax deduction. Tax savings are increased if appreciated securities are used to fund the trust because of capital gains tax considerations.

Remainder Interest in a Residence or Farm

A special agreement can be devised that permits the owner of a personal residence or farm to give the property to the Shrine while still retaining a "life estate" in the property-that is, the right to continue to use and enjoy it. The donor receives a current charitable deduction and escapes potential capital gain tax on the appreciation.

Cabrini Connections Newsletter: Page 2

Cabrini Connections Newsletter (continued)

7

Mother Cabrini Legacy Society

To enroll in the Society please fill out and return this non-binding
*Letter of Intent

_____ I/We have made a provision

_____ I/We will make a provision to include Mother Cabrini Shrine in Golden, Colorado

Through:

_____ A bequest in my/our will(s)   _____ A trust, annuity or other life income gift

_____ A life insurance policy   _____ Other means

_____ Retirement Plans   _____ Please call me so we can discuss further

Name:

Address:

City, State, Zip:

Daytime Phone: Signature & Date:

Please sign and mail to Mother Cabrini Shrine in the enclosed envelope.

*Letters of Intent are not legal documents and can be changed or revoked at any time.

Ways to Give... Ways to Give... Ways to Give

CURRENT GIFTS

The following gift arrangements will serve to support today's programs and projects of the Shrine:

Endowment

Friends are encouraged to support the Shrine's General Endowment Fund or to establish a named Endowment in support of the Shrine. The principle from the fund will continue to grow as only the annual earnings (interest) from the fund will be used.

Cash

Gifts are designated as restricted or unrestricted. Unrestricted gifts enable us to respond flexibly and quickly to immediate needs and new opportunities. These funds help seed new programs and other initiatives.

Restricted gifts will be used to support specific and designated projects of Mother Cabrini Shrine. Endowment funds may be created to preserve the long time impact of specific programs and projects.

Securities

Gifts of appreciated securities provide immediate benefit to the Shrine and, in many cases, tax deductions for the donor. Capital gains taxes can be avoided and, often, the full-market value of appreciated securities can be deducted if they have been held for longer than twelve months.

Real Estate and Other Personal Property

Real property is simply real estate—a home, farm, or other land. Your home, whether a single-family home or condominium, has probably appreciated in value over the years so that its sale would result in a sizable capital gains tax. By making a gift of property to the Shrine you may be able to avoid capital gains taxes altogether. Under certain circumstances, the donor may reserve the right to continue to occupy the home for a specified number of years or for the donor's lifetime and still receive a charitable deduction. Gifts of tangible personal property, such as art, antiques, rare books or coins, stamps, jewelry or other objects, offer another way of giving.

Charitable Lead Trusts

Assets that generate an income or that are likely to appreciate substantially can be put to good use as the principal of a charitable lead trust. A lead trust transfers the income from these assets to the Shrine for a designated period of time (typically 10 to 20 years or more). At the end of that time, the assets are returned to the donor, his or her heirs, or any other persons designated. In this manner, donors can direct a sizeable amount of annual income to the Shrine, while guaranteeing that their heirs will ultimately benefit from the asset.

Cabrini Connections Newsletter: Page 3

Cabrini Connections Newsletter (continued)

Mother Cabrini Legacy Society: Membership Benefits ⑧

The world is too small.

"There is room for everyone, for every inclination."

(Mother Cabrini)

<u>Create your own legacy:</u>

- Everyone can participate
- Annual luncheon honoring and recognizing members
- Partner with a Missionary Sister
- *Receive Cabrini Connections* newsletters
- Information and education on charitable giving and estate planning topics
- Special membership momento

A message from the Missionary Sisters of the Sacred Heart of Jesus:

As we enter the new millennium the number of our Sisters is becoming fewer and fewer. Yet the scope of our works are becoming greater and greater. Sisters and laity take on this responsibility together — making the continuation of the Cabrini mission possible all over the world.

Our commitment is to provide a continuum of services of healing, teaching, caring and giving, with a particular focus on women, children and immigrants most in need.

Mother Cabrini said: *"The world is too small to contain God's love."*

Together, we seek to make the world even smaller by connecting and involving people, inviting them to make the Cabrini legacy their own and to impart it to future generations.

We are on the road to the future. We'd like you to join us on the journey.

Will you walk this road with us?

Sr. Lucille Souza, MSC - Chairperson, Cabrini Mission Foundation

MOTHER CABRINI SHRINE
20189 Cabrini Blvd.
Golden, CO 80401

Phone: 303-526-0758
Fax: 303-526-9795

REACHING OUT TO THE HEART OF THE WORLD

Cabrini Connections Newsletter: Page 4

13

Identify Your Audience

As important as creating a bequest brochure is determining who you will send it to. Investing in a broad mailing to everyone on your mailing list can introduce your new bequest society to a wide audience. But if you lack the resources, you'll need to target your audience.

1) Target by age if you have the capability. Donors fifty years old or older are a good place to start.
2) Target by history of giving. Typically, those who have been giving for five years or more and those who make the largest gifts.
3) Individuals who have been regularly involved with your organization as volunteer leaders and donors, regardless of the size of their gifts.
4) Older individuals without children and surviving spouses.
5) Members of your volunteer committees (auxiliaries, event committees, and general volunteers).

As you decide who to put on your mailing list, take care to avoid the following myths.

• *People who make small gifts aren't prospects for bequests*

This simply isn't true. Many "smaller donors" don't have the current means to provide a $5,000 or $10,000 annual gift, even though they admire your organization and are philanthropically inclined. Their bequest gift could very well be 100 or 1000 times greater than their current income allows.

• *Only the elderly make bequests*

On the contrary, a recent study by the National Council on Planned Giving found that *more than 50 percent of the identified bequest donors were under the age of 60 and 28 percent were under the age of 45.* Including younger donors in your mailings will help you strengthen your relationship.

• *Lapsed donors should be removed from your mailing list*

Don't automatically rule out those who haven't given in recent years. Our colleague Wayne tells a cautionary tale. He was surprised when one of these lapsed donors, a woman who upon her husband's death felt she couldn't continue her annual support, left the organization with a significant bequest. In her mind, she wasn't a lapsed donor. She was simply delaying her gift.

• *Only the wealthy make bequests*

As we've said, bequests (from assets) allow donors to give much larger gifts than they can during their lifetime. While wealth and income are factors, a deep connection to your organization and belief in its mission are the key indicators of a potential gift.

14

Additional Marketing Strategies

Never assume that one message is enough to break though the clutter of communications our potential and current donors receive weekly. The key is not only crafting the message, but getting it out – often!

While your bequest brochure is a great vehicle for early marketing, relying on it solely is a bad idea. To ensure your program's success, you'll need other strategies:

1) *Make phone calls*

Focus on those donors who have made frequent, if small, gifts to you, especially in the last five years. If you've recently sent the brochure, call to ask if there are questions. Consider this: if you commit to making just two phone calls each day, you will have reached out to forty donors in your first month with the potential of reaching more than 400 by year's end. When you do call, be sure to cover the following points:

• Thank the donor for his or her past support. Of course.

• Ask if the bequest brochure was received and are there any questions.

• Ask what makes your organization special to the person?

• Ask whether he or she has considered making a bequest to your organization?

• If the person has already named you in their will, let him or her know you look forward to their being a part of your bequest society. If the timing is right, mention upcoming society events.

2) *Use your organization's publications and website*

Brief reminders about the opportunity for bequest giving can be included in your newsletter, stationery, and annual reports. You might also update your website to include a brief message that links to more detailed information on making a bequest.

3) *Meet with local professionals*

In a large city, it's impossible to capture all the professionals, but in a smaller community you should be able to identify most of the advisors who appear to be working with many of your donors. Your goal isn't to review their client lists, but rather to familiarize these professionals with your bequest society. Attorneys serving on your board will be helpful in this regard; and based on your relationship with several key donors you might be able to learn from them who's doing the most estate planning work in town.

Not only can local professional advisors serve as a resource for your ongoing questions, but they can be excellent ambassadors by introducing or acknowledging their familiarity with your organization when their client suggests an interest.

Ideally, try to meet with at least one insurance agent, accountant, and estate attorney. Inviting estate planning attorneys to a special cultivation lunch can be helpful, but include as well certified public accountants, personal attorneys, investment managers, trust officers, and others you feel it would be good to know.

4) *Print gift receipt reminders*

Include a reminder on all gift receipts and thank you letters inviting donors to consider joining your bequest society. The back of any return envelope is also a good place to begin a conversation by including the following check boxes:

- I have included [*your organization*] in my will. Please send me information about membership in the Legacy society.
- Please send me information about bequests.
- Please send me information about [*your organization's*] legacy society.

5) *Include articles in your organization's newsletter*

Place a short "advertisement" of the program and contact information in each issue of your newsletter. The sample shown on the next page provides information as well as a tear-off card to return.

6) *Send regular information on bequests and estate planning*

There are two principal approaches here:

A. Mail a Bi-Annual Bequest Letter

Twice a year, send a mailing to all your bequest prospects. Include informational articles on bequests, as well as a feature article on a current donor. Of course, be sure to include information on how to join your bequest society.

B. Create a Bequest Society Newsletter.

This is a much larger undertaking, so we've devoted the next chapter to this marketing tool.

Bequest newsletter page

Legacy Society Update
Planned Giving Helps Secure the Future of
Mother Cabrini High School

One of the many charitable gift giving options available to donors is planned giving. Planned giving not only benefits the charitable organization but allows the donor to develop a financial plan for benefiting his or her future.

Available through Mother Cabrini High School to all alumnae free of charge is an at home ten-week creative estate planning course that outlines many planned giving options. This course provides information about how to gain maximum benefits from investments, real property, other holdings and advice about creative gift planning. There is no obligation to any gift giving program by participating in this free educational course. For more information about how to acquire course material call Kathy Muskopf in the Advancement Office at (212) 923-9114.

We remain grateful especially to those alumnae who have already included Mother Cabrini High School in their planned giving. These gifts help ensure the future of Mother Cabrini High School and St. Frances Xavier Cabrini's educational legacy.

Legacy Society

❑ *Please send me more information about the Legacy Society.*
❑ *Please send me more information about planning my estate.*
❑ *I'm considering a gift to Mother Cabrini High School, please call me.*

The best time to call is_____ a.m/p.m.

I've already included Mother Cabrini High School in my estate plan through

❑ *my will*
❑ *a trust arrangement*
❑ *an insurance policy*
❑ *other_____*

Name: _____

Address:_____

_____

Telephone: _____

Email: _____

The Cabrinian Spring 2006

A page from the bequest newsletter of Mother Cabrini High School, providing information and an easy tear-off card for the reader.

15

The Bequest Society Newsletter

In addition to introducing your new program with a brochure, a bequest newsletter works well as an ongoing marketing tool.

You have a threefold purpose here: to provide information on recent members, to offer topical articles on estate planning, and to give donors yet another opportunity to alert you if they've made a bequest. The newsletter can be sent four to six months after the bequest society mailing and to the same audience.

The letter shown on the next page can be used as a template, but you'll want to personalize it for your own organization and donor.

Dear Sarah,

I've enclosed our inaugural copy of *Future Matters*. This special newsletter will keep you informed of useful, up-to-date financial and estate planning ideas. In coming issues, we'll also feature many of our dear friends who have informed us that they, too, have made a bequest in their will to benefit those we serve.

Future Matters will also focus on the variety of ways you can save on income taxes through charitable giving.

We know providing for your family, loved ones and charitable organizations is a priority for you. We hope you will find this and subsequent issues to be a handy source of valuable information on efficient and effective ways to fulfill your wishes.

If you have any questions on any of the material covered in the newsletter, feel free to contact me or return the reply card. I welcome your comments and suggestions. Perhaps we can talk over lunch soon. I'll give you a call next week.

Having you as our friend and supporter means so much to us. If we can be of assistance in any way, please let me know.

Sincerely,

When sending your newsletter to new donors thanking them for their recent bequest, be sure to include a personalized letter such as the one shown here.

■ **What to include in your newsletter**

In your newsletter you'll want to include the following:

1) How to make a bequest

2) Contact information at your organization

3) A self-addressed postcard or tear-off that the reader can send back to inform you of a gift or to request additional information

4) A listing of current society members (with their permission, of course)

5) A profile of one of your members

6) Educational information about charitable bequests and – as your bequest society grows – other planned giving options if you offer them

7) Timely information on bequest giving (such as changes in estate laws or tax deductions)

■ **In-house or outside production?**

Using the above information, you may be comfortable producing your own newsletter. Certainly this is cost-effective. And, in fact, the less-polished look may appeal to a number of your donors.

At the same time, there are advantages to having a professional firm produce your newsletter, assuming you have the financial resources. Among them are the following:

1. You'll have access to a range of 'stock' articles on estate planning, charitable bequests, and the like.

2. You'll have the option of including your own text, pictures, and stories to personalize your brochure.

3. You'll have a consultant who has done this before and can provide guidance as to what works and what doesn't.

4. Depending on the size of your organization's marketing resources, this outside-produced piece may provide a "professional look" some donors prefer.

How often you send your newsletter will largely be determined by your budget. In any case, a minimum of one mailing per year, in addition to the bequest mailing discussed previously, will be a good start. Over time, you might increase the frequency of your newsletter mailings to two, three, or four times yearly.

On the following pages, we're including a sample produced by an outside firm. You'll find another in the appendix.

Bequest Society Newsletter

CENTRAL OHIO RADIO READING SERVICE

CARING VOICES

INSIDE

Savvy Estate Planning: Where To Leave Your Retirement Plan

SOUTH FAMILY NAMES CORRS AS BENEFICIARY

For Ellen Kallos, CORRS was an essential, daily need. "It kept her going, kept her alive, kept her mind sharp," her daughter, Cindy South, explains. Prior to being diagnosed with macular degeneration, Ellen was an avid reader. "She read every word of the newspaper every day," Cindy says. When she began to lose her vision, she learned about CORRS at the Vision Center of Central Ohio. "[It became] her connection to everyday life." CORRS also met another important need of companionship: "She had people who she listened to who became like friends." Other readers provided inspiration. "She would hear someone on the radio and [later] find out they were blind. She learned that she shouldn't feel visually impaired...

Ellen Kallos and daughter Cindy South

> **"SHE READ**
> EVERY WORD OF THE
> NEWSPAPER EVERY DAY."
>
> —Cindy South

The day before she died, I walked in to find her holding a cane in one hand, and the vacuum cleaner in the other."

Deeply touched by the role CORRS played in her mother's life, Cindy and her husband, Rod, named CORRS as a beneficiary in their will. "There are so many types of charities, and you don't always see how they benefit someone else on a daily basis," Cindy says, "[but] we know CORRS will continue to...help people." Their gift makes them the newest members of the CORRS Legacy Society.

We are also happy to announce the other members of our Legacy Society: Brenda Burris, Bill Cooper, Dick and Fran Luckay, Penny Procter and Steve Miller, Mary Alice Demas, Stephen Miller, and several anonymous friends.

For more information, please contact Sandy Turner at (614) 274-7650 or David Valinsky, planned giving volunteer, at (614) 485-1246.

Central Ohio Radio Reading Services: Page 1

Bequest Society Newsletter (continued)

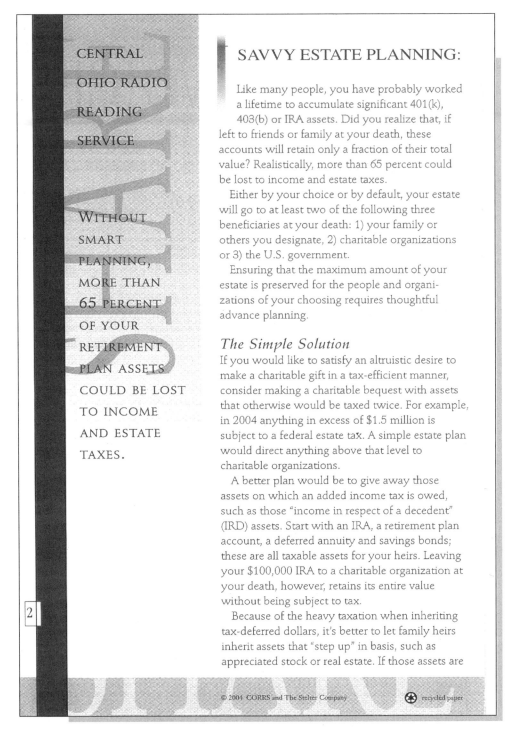

CENTRAL OHIO RADIO READING SERVICE

WITHOUT SMART PLANNING, MORE THAN 65 PERCENT OF YOUR RETIREMENT PLAN ASSETS COULD BE LOST TO INCOME AND ESTATE TAXES.

2

SAVVY ESTATE PLANNING:

Like many people, you have probably worked a lifetime to accumulate significant 401(k), 403(b) or IRA assets. Did you realize that, if left to friends or family at your death, these accounts will retain only a fraction of their total value? Realistically, more than 65 percent could be lost to income and estate taxes.

Either by your choice or by default, your estate will go to at least two of the following three beneficiaries at your death: 1) your family or others you designate, 2) charitable organizations or 3) the U.S. government.

Ensuring that the maximum amount of your estate is preserved for the people and organizations of your choosing requires thoughtful advance planning.

The Simple Solution

If you would like to satisfy an altruistic desire to make a charitable gift in a tax-efficient manner, consider making a charitable bequest with assets that otherwise would be taxed twice. For example, in 2004 anything in excess of $1.5 million is subject to a federal estate tax. A simple estate plan would direct anything above that level to charitable organizations.

A better plan would be to give away those assets on which an added income tax is owed, such as those "income in respect of a decedent" (IRD) assets. Start with an IRA, a retirement plan account, a deferred annuity and savings bonds; these are all taxable assets for your heirs. Leaving your $100,000 IRA to a charitable organization at your death, however, retains its entire value without being subject to tax.

Because of the heavy taxation when inheriting tax-deferred dollars, it's better to let family heirs inherit assets that "step up" in basis, such as appreciated stock or real estate. If those assets are

Central Ohio Radio Reading Services: Page 2

Bequest Society Newsletter (continued)

WHERE TO LEAVE YOUR RETIREMENT PLAN

sold later, there won't be much of an income tax due. This proactive approach is more tax efficient—the charitable organization receives more, heirs keep more and the IRS gets nothing.

Benefits for You and Us

For owners of significant retirement plans, naming a charitable remainder trust (CRT) as beneficiary might make better financial sense. While there's usually no charitable *income* tax deduction, there's often a significant *estate* tax deduction. In addition, the CRT can receive the entire retirement plan distribution without paying current income tax, as well as ensure a steady income stream for a surviving spouse.

For older heirs, the CRT funded with IRD assets is an ideal way to reduce required payments from a retirement plan and spread them over longer payout periods than may otherwise be possible.

Make Your Wishes Clear

Without changes in beneficiary designations or specific language in your will, however, your estate can't make charitable gifts of IRD assets. Bequests in a will or testamentary trust are generally satisfied with cash or other readily available assets and not necessarily with assets that have a tax liability.

These types of gifts can be relatively complex, so consult with competent professional advisors to make sure gifts of IRD assets are properly implemented.

If you would like to ensure that Central Ohio Radio Reading Service benefits from your hard-earned assets, give us a call for a no-obligation consultation. We will help you and your advisor design a plan that will benefit everyone involved.

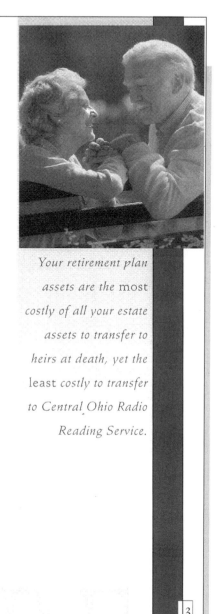

Your retirement plan assets are the most *costly of all your estate assets to transfer to heirs at death, yet the* least *costly to transfer to Central Ohio Radio Reading Service.*

3

Central Ohio Radio Reading Services: Page 3

Bequest Society Newsletter (continued)

Giving Back

After accumulating wealth and assets for a lifetime, your focus now shifts to the best way to distribute retirement accounts to your chosen charitable organizations.

Be sure to request the free brochure, A New Use for Your Retirement Plan Assets.

To receive your copy, complete and return the enclosed response card/reply mailer.

TRUSTS—A VERSATILE TOOL FOR PLANNING AHEAD

A trust is a legal arrangement by which an individual passes ownership of property to a trustee for the benefit of named beneficiaries, individuals or charitable organizations.

Trusts are widely used today to pass property to heirs, or charitable organizations, manage property, avoid probate and save taxes. Trusts created during life are private. They do not become a matter of public record as do probated wills, and their terms are more difficult to challenge than the terms of a will.

Revocable trusts, often called living trusts, have the advantage of flexibility, even dissolution, but they do not save on taxes. They become irrevocable, however, after the death of the grantor. Only then do the provisions of the trust instrument rule. There can be disappointments but no changes.

Irrevocable trusts are more rigid and usually cannot be changed, but they offer favorable tax benefits. Think of the trust as a contract between you and the trustee.

Because trusts are specifically designed, carefully thought-out, less subject to challenge, less expensive and more quickly distributed than probated property, they may best serve your planning for tomorrow.

CENTRAL OHIO RADIO READING SERVICE

2955 West Broad Street
Columbus, OH 43204
(614) 274-7650
Fax: (614) 274-9340

4

Central Ohio Radio Reading Services: Page 4

16

Follow Up on Responses

As your bequest program gets underway, you'll begin receiving responses from current and potential donors. It's essential to stay connected with these individuals with regular (and timely) communication.

• Current donors

Keeping in touch with this group is critical, and personal visits are the best way to do so. Not only will you learn more about their individual interests and motivations, but they can provide you with special testimonial stories for your newsletter and story ideas for your brochure and annual report.

• Those who are connected to your organization (auxiliary members, volunteers, docents, grateful patients, alumni) but who haven't named you in their will.

In virtually all situations, visiting with your donors one-on-one will be the most effective way to introduce your program and secure bequests. But it may not always be possible. A second option is to hold a special event (a simple luncheon will do) to introduce your program to groups such as volunteers, retirees, docents, and friends. Invite organizational leadership (executive director, CEO, board chair) to provide a warm welcome. You might also consider inviting a special guest to ensure good attendance (see Appendix for a sample agenda).

Whatever you do, *remember to tell those present that you're interested in knowing if they've left your organization in their will!* Some people don't know that you're interested in being informed.

One of our colleagues happily learned this lesson at one of her luncheons. Following her remarks, she struck up a conversation with one of the attendees. Lo and behold, he says to her: "I've named your group in my will ... for $3.5 million. If I had known you wanted to know, I would have mentioned it sooner." She did what any of us would do: took a deep breath, thanked John for his gift, and frantically began searching for the executive director.

• Those who have asked for information or informed you that your organization is named in their will.

Call these individuals. In addition to thanking them, ask why they're involved and what they like about the organization. You may find they want to be further involved. You might also learn of a special interest they have that dovetails with a project you need funding for.

If they don't already have a bequest society brochure, suggest that you can deliver it in person. Or if you do mail it, be sure to include a special note.

For those requesting information, be prompt in replying. In fact, it's a good idea to call before sending the information to confirm their wishes.

Once you have responded, follow up with a phone call in two to four weeks.

As for what to do when you receive notification from an attorney that you have been named as a beneficiary by an individual who has recently passed away, turn to the next chapter.

17

You've Just Been Notified of a Matured Bequest: Now What?

Believe it or not, one day all of your work will pay off.

The phone will ring, and the individual on the other end will tell you your organization has been named in the will of a woman whose name you neither recognize nor know anything about.

Now what?

It's really quite simple:

1) Clarify that the gift has matured (that the donor is deceased), and ask whether any other organizations are a part of the gift. Calling the professional advisor is simply a matter of due process. Beyond that, you may learn that several organizations are recipients of a simultaneous gift. If so, knowing this ahead of time may allow you to pool resources and offer more elaborate recognition (with the family's

blessing, of course).

2) Determine what relationship, if any, the donor had with your organization. Was she a patient, a regular visitor to the museum, a devoted theatre-goer? This may help shape the recognition you provide.

3) Identify any family members and determine if it's appropriate to communicate with them. In addition to being a matter of respect, the family might also provide a moving story you can incorporate into your promotional materials.

4) Once you understand the donor's history with your organization, it may be appropriate to discuss the following with a family member:

- Are there recommendations on how the funds should be used?
- Can we inspire others with a story about the donor?
- How would you feel about our announcing the donor's gift?
- Is there a special way to recognize the donor?

Often, family members will be honored that you want to recognize their loved one. But there will be times when they'll reject any limelight – for themselves and the donor. Regardless, contacting the family early is the right thing to do.

18

Ten Final Thoughts

While no single book can hope to cover everything you need to know about raising money through bequests, we hope we've supplied the tools to get you started. Regardless of how elaborate or simple your program, these last thoughts will be central to your success. Cut them out, paste them on a wall, and read them often.

1) It's the frequency of regular gifts, not the size that indicates a potential bequest donor.

2) Don't overlook lapsed donors. If you have the resources, keep them on your bequest mailing list and send them annual reports.

3) Never underestimate the potential of donors based on their appearance, zip code, or the square footage of their house. Remember: even if they aren't *The Millionaire Next Door*, they could bequeath a $50,000 to $100,000 gift.

4) Follow up, follow up, follow up. Make the phone call when an

interested party inquires about your bequest society.

5) New members to your bequest society should be thanked often and by several key people such as the CEO, board chair, and head of the appropriate department.

6) Selected phone calls to your bequest society members just to say, "Hi, thanks again, and here are some new things going on..." will pay great dividends.

7) Keep your optimism even when bequest responses don't flow in like major gifts, because they won't. It's commonly acknowledged that:

- More than 40% of adults *don't* have a current will. These individuals have to be educated first, and that requires time.
- Of those who have named your organization as a beneficiary, 60 to 70 percent won't inform you.
- Whenever you send bequest mailings, you'll receive VERY few responses.
- Often, people will take a long time to finally determine what type of bequest they want to make.
- Donors can always change their minds and remove your organization from their will – however, fewer than 10 percent actually do.

8) Often, the top leaders of our organizations are more focused on annual gifts than deferred gifts. Make it your business to invite, encourage, and ask all of your staff and volunteer leaders to become members of your bequest society.

9) Don't hesitate because you don't know all the technical and legal aspects of bequest giving. Your energy and ability to develop a relationship are far more important – you can rent, buy, or learn the other.

10) If you're not out there inviting a donor to join your bequest society, be assured that other organizations are.

19

Trust Your Instincts

Well, if you've gotten this far, we hope you've found some nuggets, insights, or guidelines that are helpful as you begin or continue your journey with bequest fundraising.

If we've learned anything in our decades of doing this work, it's this: no book will ever teach you everything about this incredible world of philanthropy. Times change, every donor is different, and frankly, there aren't any hard and fast rules.

■ **Except one** ...

Trust your instincts.

In the end, it will be you and the donor – and perhaps a dedicated volunteer – making small talk at a special event, meeting in an office on the twentieth floor, or sitting across a kitchen table, sharing tea and stories while you look at old photo albums. After all the presentations and brochures and newsletters, there will be an opportunity for you to simply ask: "Would you be willing to establish a bequest to support this project which is obviously important to you?"

The business of fundraising is the practice of attentive and well-intentioned human relations. If it feels wrong, it probably is, and if it's right ... well, those are the moments that make the long hours, stressful timetables, and difficult questions from board and staff leadership worth it all.

At that moment, you will be on your way to helping another person do their part to heal the world. And from our perspective, there's no higher calling.

APPENDIX

The Bequest Test

This questionnaire may be used with your board or bequest advisory committee members to test their level of understanding or to begin a discussion of bequests and their potential for your organization.

Approximately what percent of adult Americans do not have a will?

[ ] 25%   [ ] 40%   [ ] 65%

Approximately how much total revenue do charitable organizations in the United States earn annually from bequest giving?

[ ] $1 billion   [ ] $7 billion   [ ] $17 billion

Eighty percent of Americans contribute to nonprofit groups throughout their lifetimes. Approximately what percent of these choose to continue their support through a charitable bequest?

[ ] 4%   [ ] 6%   [ ] 8%

What is the number one reason individuals give for making charitable bequests?

_____

List three ways to promote bequests without cost:

1) _____

2) _____

3) _____

(Answers on next page)

The Bequest Test Answer Key

Approximately what percent of adult Americans do not have a will?

        [ ] 25%   [X] 40%   [ ] 65%

Approximately how much total revenue do charitable organizations in the United States earn annually from bequest giving?

        [ ] $1 billion   [ ] $7 billion   [X] $17 billion

Eighty percent of Americans contribute to nonprofit groups throughout their lifetimes. Approximately what percent of these choose to continue their support through a charitable bequest?

        [X] 4%   [ ] 6%   [ ] 8%

What is the number one reason people make charitable bequests?

They believe in the mission of the organization

List three ways to promote bequests without cost:

1) An article in your organization's newsletter

2) A reminder in a personal letter or mailing

3) A reminder note as part of your organization's stationary

Sample Language for Bequests

Sometimes, all the marketing in the world won't be as helpful as providing your donors with the tools they need to add a bequest to their wills. Have some sample language on hand for them to take to their professional advisor's office.

The Bequest

1. Cash, securities, real estate or property of any description may be bequeathed to THE ORGANIZATION by a clause in the donor's Will or by a Codicil added to the Will. The donor using this method retains full control and use of the property during his lifetime and may alter or revoke the bequest at any time.

2. At the time of the donor's death, the bequest qualifies as a charitable deduction for estate tax purposes. The bequest does not, however, provide the donor with any tax advantages during their lifetime, nor does it provide an assured income for donors or their beneficiaries, as other plans may.

The following are recommended clauses that may be used to make a gift to THE ORGANIZATION through your will. The following clauses, of course, are only examples. Be sure to contact your attorney for proper legal advice.

General Bequest

I give and bequeath _____ Dollars ($_____) to THE ORGANIZATION, a not-for-profit organization incorporated in the State of _____ the principle office at ADDRESS, for its general purposes.

Specific Bequest

I give, devise, and bequeath all my rights, title, and interest in and to [*describe the specific property*], to THE ORGANIZA-TION, a not-for-profit organization incorporated in the State of _____ the principle office at ADDRESS, for its general purposes.

Residuary Estate

I give my residuary estate, which is all the rest, residue, and remainder of my property, real and personal, of every kind and description and wherever located (including all legacies and devises that may for any reason fail to take effect), belonging to me at the time of my death or subject to my disposal by will to THE ORGANIZATION, a not-for-profit organization incorpo-rated in the State of _____ the principle office at ADDRESS, for its general purposes.

Endowment Bequest

I give, devise, and bequeath [*describe the specific property or amount*] to THE ORGANIZATION, a not-for-profit organi-zation incorporated in the State of _____, the principle office at ADDRESS, to establish an endowment fund (to be known as the _____ Fund); the principal amount to be invested and the annual income therefrom to be used for the benefit of THE ORGANIZATION.

Addition to Endowment Fund

I give, devise and bequeath to THE ORGANIZATION, a not-for-profit organization incorporated in the State of _____ and located in ADDRESS, and its successors forever, the sum of $_____ Dollars (or otherwise describe the gift) and direct that this bequest be added to the endowment fund of THE ORGANIZATION. (*Where the bequest takes this form, only the income may be used*).

Codicil

Having hereinbefore made my last Will and Testament dated and being of sound mind, I hereby make, publish and declare the following Codicil thereto: (here insert clause in same form as if it had been included in body of Will). Except as hereinbefore changed, I hereby ratify, confirm and republish my said last Will and Testament.

(We strongly recommended that the donor employ a competent lawyer to prepare the Will or Codicil and to supervise its execution in order to comply with all the requirements of the law of the state in which the maker of the Will resides, as well as the provisions of the Internal Revenue Code governing the deduction of charitable gifts and bequests. It is also wise to give the THE ORGANIZATION considerable latitude in the use of any fund so that a change of circumstances may not impair the usefulness of the gift. The President of THE ORGANIZATION will be glad upon request to review the phrasing of any proposed form of bequest, subject to your attorney's approval).

Often, donors or their professional advisors will call your organization to confirm the address or request some language that they can provide their attorney.

Suggestions for Bequest Society Names

The following names are a combination of those we've encountered over the years and our own brainstorming. Perhaps one of them will inspire you.

The Greystone Circle	The Honor Roll
The Greystone Heritage Trust	Dream Builders
The Cornerstone Society	Circle of Hope
Cornerstone Club	The Legacy of Hope
Golden Acorn	The Builders Society
Benefactor Society	The Life Line
The Heritage Society	Children's Circle
The Path Finders	Founder's Circle
The Acorn Group	Legacy Angels
Lamplighters Guild	The Eternal Flame Society
Seeds of Tomorrow Society	Brushstrokes Guild
The Mission Keepers	The Phoenix Circle
The Circle of Concern	Friends for Life
Health Investors	The Feather Society
The Impossible Dream	Redeemer Legacy Guild
The Gifts for Life Society	Painting the Future Society
President's Circle	The Mustard Seed Society

Sample Bequest/Planned Giving Newsletter

A FINANCIAL AND CHARITABLE GUIDE FROM BON SECOURS COTTAGE HEALTH SERVICES

SUMMER 2006

Future Matters

Inside

- Seven Costly Estate Planning Fallacies • Financial Philosophies for Families
- Leaving an Eternal Legacy

Partners in Outreach

Through a planned gift to Bon Secours Cottage Health Services, you become a valuable vested partner in our mission to serve and to excel in our outreach to others.

BON SECOURS COTTAGE HEALTH SERVICES *Henry Ford HEALTH SYSTEM*

Friends,

We are delighted to present this first issue of *Future Matters* to you, our friends and supporters of Bon Secours Cottage Health Services (BSCHS). As health care continues to change at a breakneck pace, the mission of BSCHS remains constant: "To provide good help to those in need." This good help is made possible every day through the care and concern of every nurse, physician and staff member of our organization. It is also made possible through the generous philanthropy of community-minded citizens like you. Without this generosity, there can be no mission.

The Bon Secours Cottage Health Services Foundation was founded three short years ago to ensure that the mission and values of our organizations continue on for future generations. The Foundation board of directors, made up of members of our communities, work tirelessly to seek out new funding opportunities to build new facilities and new programs for the benefit of all who come through our doors. Since the inception of the Joint Venture, more than $16 million has been raised in the areas of women's health, cancer, emergency medicine and now the latest project—the renovation and expansion of a new ICU/Critical Care Unit at Bon Secours Hospital.

Within these pages you will learn of estate tax–saving strategies, as well as opportunities for retirement planning regardless of your age, profession or cumulative wealth. In fact, since the founding of BSCHS in 1998, more than $6 million has been received from generous friends after their lifetimes. You will read on the back of this publication about one such individual in the person of Monsignor Francis X. Canfield, longtime leader of St. Paul's parish and friend to so many in our communities.

We hope on this, the 125th anniversary of the Sisters of Bon Secours in the United States, that you also will consider a planned gift for the good help of future generations and the mission, which remains central to all we do.

Hugo S. Higbie, Chairman
Sr. Patricia Heath, President

Bon Secours Cottage Health Services
Bequest/Planned Giving Newsletter: Page 1

Seven Costly Estate Planning Fallacies

Should your estate plan cause you concern? Maybe you already have an estate plan—but how old is it? Perhaps you made a will years ago and you're satisfied that is all you need. If you're married, is joint ownership all that is necessary? If you're single, you may feel you don't have to plan. As individuals consider their estate plans, a number of common misconceptions surface. Here are some blunders that can plague your loved ones—and ways to avoid them:

> Becoming proactive in your estate planning will result in a better outcome for everyone involved.

1. *"I already have a will."* Unlike art and antiques, a will doesn't improve with age. The passage of time presents unanticipated circumstances, such as a divorce or remarriage, a new child or grandchild, revised tax laws, a move to another state, valuable new assets—and current plans to support the hospital. This could be the right moment to put new life into your timeworn will.

2. *"Everything's joint."* Joint ownership seems ideal because it helps to avoid probate and expedites the survivor's access. But joint title may also inflict unnecessary tax burdens and upset trust plans. For example, a bypass trust won't be funded with property that's jointly owned. To sidestep title traps, consult with your attorney.

3. *"I'm single, so I don't need an estate plan."* But who will benefit from your estate—and in what amounts? Perhaps you have children, grandchildren or good friends to consider. Beyond these concerns, you may have greater freedom now to remember us in your will, such as endowing your annual gift to us with a reliable flow of funds.

4. *"My will covers everything."* Not necessarily. Your retirement assets may never reach your rightful heirs if you've failed to update beneficiary designation forms. They trump your will when it comes to passing along your 401(k), IRAs and life insurance policies. Complete new forms so that old forms won't leave these assets to a dead parent or ex-spouse. If you have charitable goals, making us beneficiary of a retirement plan can cut the taxes on your family's inheritance.

5. *"No death tax? Then I don't need a trust plan."* Larger exclusions from the federal estate tax diminish the incentive for tax-savings trusts. Yet there are numerous family and philanthropic situations in which trusts remain valuable estate planning strategies. And long after your lifetime, your trust plan makes sure your money will be conserved and prudently invested for your chosen heirs.

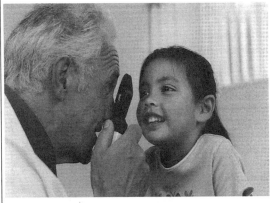

Bon Secours Cottage Health Services
Bequest/Planned Giving Newsletter: Page 2

Sample Bequest/Planned Giving Newsletter

6. *"My affairs are in good hands."*
   Say you have a fine lawyer—but who is your executor or personal administrator? This fiduciary should have the experience to gather assets, pay creditors, manage investments, file tax returns, satisfy legacies and account to your beneficiaries. And if you create trusts, make sure you've named a trustee who can prudently manage the trust assets.

7. *"I worry more about myself, not my heirs."* A good estate plan should also bear in mind your current needs. One solution for our supporters is a charitable remainder trust funded with highly appreciated long-term stocks that currently payout low dividends. You'll benefit from higher income and a sizable tax deduction.
   Even with good intentions, sometimes common errors can result in unnecessary hurt feelings. Becoming proactive in your estate planning will result in a better outcome for everyone involved.

Financial Philosophies for Families

The seeds of charitable giving are not automatically planted at birth. Philanthropic individuals must learn, usually over a long period of time, the values that inspire their donations. Often, the values we learn at home are those that grow into a philosophy in life.

Most important, a family financial philosophy starts with the care of family members, addressing such basic needs as the mortgage, medical costs and tuition bills.

But most of us—and we rarely take the time to ponder this issue—actually do earn or possess more than we need. Though the definition of "need" is highly personal, the value system we learn as we grow prompts our desire to help others. After all, not all wealthy people are charitable, and not all charitable people are wealthy. The difference then is clearly not the amount of available money. Instead, the measure of compassion for others makes all the difference in the world.

The foundation of philanthropy often originates from our faith—where we learn to support others—but regardless of faith, everyone can employ the philosophy of helping others. Compassion lies within the heart of each of us. We need only to find the key.

Plant Your Charitable Seedlings

One	Two	Three
Annual gifts ensure that we will be able to provide much-needed services to the community every year.	A major gift this year lets us apply those funds to support immediate projects.	A bequest in your will demonstrates your commitment to future generations.

♻ printed on recycled paper

Bon Secours Cottage Health Services
Bequest/Planned Giving Newsletter: Page 3

Sample Bequest/Planned Giving Newsletter

Leaving an Eternal Legacy

In Loving Memory of

Msgr. Francis X. Canfield
1920-1998

Friend, shepherd, confessor, avid tennis enthusiast and major benefactor all describe Monsignor Francis X. Canfield, former head of St. Paul Parish, Grosse Pointe.

For more than 25 years, Father, then Monsignor, Canfield watched over and helped turn St. Paul Parish more outward than ever before. The spiritual life of the parish experienced the ecumenism and new light that came forth from Vatican II. Changing demographics of the community forced new decisions in the direction of the school, forcing closure of the high school to make way for the burgeoning population of grade-schoolers. In 1978, a raging fire ruined the interior of the historic church, and it was under Monsignor Canfield's skilled guidance that the parish stepped forward and generously restored the church in eight months' time. In retirement, he founded the American Friends of the Vatican Library while he presided as rector of the Sacred Heart Seminary. His greatest legacy was yet to unfold.

In March of 1995, Monsignor Canfield made an anonymous major gift to the Bon Secours of Michigan Foundation. His gift established the Monsignor Francis X. Canfield Endowment for Bioethical Considerations. The program provides ongoing education for the Bon Secours medical staff and community on current and relevant issues in bioethics, particularly as they impact community health care and well-being.

> Monsignor Canfield's gift to the Bon Secours of Michigan Foundation established an endowment for bioethical considerations that provides ongoing education for medical staff and the community.

BON SECOURS COTTAGE HEALTH SERVICES *Henry Ford* HEALTH SYSTEM

John Danaher, CEO, Foundation | Vice President, Philanthropy
159 Kercheval
Grosse Pointe Farms, MI 48236
(313) 640-2540 | Fax (313) 640-2505

www.bshsi.org

Bon Secours Cottage Health Services
Bequest/Planned Giving Newsletter: Page 4

Sample Response Card

Leave Behind More Than Memories—Create a Legacy

❑ Please send me the FREE brochure, Planning for Your Life, Your Will, Your Heirs.

❑ Please provide me with more information about estate planning

❑ I have a question. Please call me. Best time to call: _____ a.m./p.m.

❑ I have not previously informed you, but I have already included you in my estate plan through:

    ❑ my will ❑ a trust arrangement ❑ an insurance policy ❑ my retirement plan assets

    ❑ other _____

Name (Please print.) _____

Telephone _____

Address _____

E-mail _____

City, State, ZIP _____

This information is strictly confidential.

Sample Agenda for Introducing a Bequest Program

A special event, such as a luncheon, can be effective in introducing your bequest program to groups of potential donors. While the sample below is specifically targeted to a hospital setting, it can be adapted for any organization.

I. WELCOME

The president or CEO of the hospital thanks everyone for coming and for their volunteer service. He or she should also recognize and thank the members of the bequest advisory committee and give a brief explanation of why the bequest program is important in the larger context of the hospital's work.

II. THE DOCTOR IS IN

Invite one or two cherished physicians (active or retired) to speak of their experiences at the hospital. Not only will they provide a 'draw' for people to attend, but they can share heartfelt experiences about the impact of the hospital and thus, of bequests made in its support.

III. THE BEQUEST SOCIETY

The volunteer head of the bequest advisory committee (or someone from the development staff) talks about the bequest society itself: how bequests benefit the hospital, how to join, and the benefits of membership. The speaker may also want to recognize any significant bequest donors in attendance. Also, be sure to have all bequest society members listed in the program.

IV. ANSWER QUESTIONS

Reserve ample time for this portion of the program as it will often prove to be the most beneficial in educating those who are considering this special commitment. Lastly, leave time at the end for socializing. Some people who aren't comfortable asking questions in a large group will seek out the committee members and staff. And who knows – this may be when you learn of an incredible gift.

Sample Case for Support

ST. MARY'S MEDICAL CENTER FOUNDATION
HUNTINGTON, WEST VIRGINIA

ST. MARY'S LEGACY SOCIETY CASE FOR SUPPORT

A hospital never sleeps. The demanding business of caring for the sick and the injured goes on 24 hours a day, seven days a week at St. Mary's Medical Center. But the rhythm of that care slows in the late night and early morning, when the day's visitors are gone and the center is left to its trained staff and those over whom they so carefully keep watch.

The hours tick slowly by. Finally, dawn nears. Outside, the first rays of sun soon appear, and inside, the medical center's public address system crackles to life: "Good morning and welcome to St. Mary's Medical Center. May we pause for a few moments of prayer and reflection as we begin our day together.

"God, thank you for the gift of this day and for all the gifts that we will share with each other. May the gifts of healing, of hospitality and hope be in this place. We ask for your peace for all our patients and family. Through your love may the joy of life be given to all who come here. ... Amen."

It's the beginning of another day at St. Mary's Medical Center. Another day that will be filled with tears and laughter, with love and concern, with compassion and caring. Especially caring.

- James E. Casto

A Tradition of Faith, Hope, Healing and Service

On November 6, 1924, the Sisters of the Pallottine Missionary Society opened St. Mary's Hospital. From the moment they first opened its doors, the Sisters set out to fulfill their mission: *We are inspired by the love of Christ to provide quality health care in ways which respect the God-given dignity of each person and the sacredness of human life.*

So began the tradition that is St. Mary's Medical Center. It's been more than eight decades since the doors first opened and, during that time, thousands of lay people have joined the Sisters in fulfilling the medical center's mission. Since then, St. Mary's has continued to build on its tradition of faith, hope, healing and service.

The Tri State's Community Hospital

When the Pallottine Missionary Sisters first arrived in the United States from Bremerhaven, Germany, the city of Huntington had nearly a dozen hospitals, but all were privately owned, most were small (some had only 10 or 12 beds) and none were, in any sense of the word, a community hospital. When they opened the new, 35-bed hospital, their first patient was a charity case, beginning the hospital's long tradition of caring for the poor.

From these humble beginnings, St. Mary's has grown into a true community hospital, serving patients from 20 counties in three states, and remaining committed to caring for all of its patients, regardless of their ability to pay. Today, St. Mary's is a large tertiary care medical facility, Cabell County's largest private employer (2,200+ employees) and, at 393 beds, one of the largest healthcare facilities in West Virginia. In the tradition of the Pallottine Missionary Sisters, the medical center's mission remains focused on the sacredness of human life and the God-given dignity of all those who walk through its doors, regardless of their ability to pay. Advanced medical care delivered with compassion is the hallmark of St. Mary's reputation.

State-of-the-Art Medical Care Close to Home

Our community counts on St. Mary's for exceptional medical services provided by caring professionals. This commitment to the highest quality medical care is evident in our centers of excellence in cardiac care, cancer care, neuroscience and emergency/trauma service. We provide the latest in cutting-edge technology, from our Regional Heart Institute, where we perform thousands of cardiac procedures annually, to our Regional Neuroscience Center, where complex, life-saving procedures are performed on the brain and spine.

§ For more than 40 years, <u>St. Mary's Regional Cancer Center</u> has been on the front lines of the battle with cancer. St. Mary's provides a full range of radiation, medical and surgical oncology services.

§ The majority of neurosurgical procedures in Huntington are performed at <u>St. Mary's Regional Neuroscience Center</u>, which features a primary stroke center with a disease-specific certification from the Joint Commission on Accreditation of Healthcare Organizations.

§ <u>St. Mary's Regional Heart Institute</u> is the Tri-State's most experienced comprehensive cardiac care program. The institute's cardiologists and cardiothoracic surgeons specialize in both invasive and non-invasive procedures.

Tradition of Excellence in Healthcare Education

St. Mary's Medical Center is proud of its role as the only medical center in West Virginia to own and operate a School of Nursing, School of Radiography and School of Respiratory Care.

At St. Mary's Schools of Nursing, Radiography and Respiratory Care, we're committed to the hospital-based educational model. Our skilled faculty offers quality instruction, and immediate access to the facilities and staff of St. Mary's Medical Center gives students direct patient experience beginning in their first semester. They are able to put theory into practice using state-of-the-art equipment in a variety of real-life settings. At the same time, in keeping with our hospital mission, we teach the importance of compassionate care, ensuring that tomorrow's professionals foster a deep respect for the sacredness of all life.

A Legacy of Care

Throughout its history, St. Mary's Medical Center has built on the traditions of faith, hope, healing and service. Yet the underlying foundation of these traditions has been that of care. The desire to build on these traditions through further expansion and growth of our healthcare mission is why we created the new St. Mary's Legacy Society.

How can you demonstrate your own commitment to the health of future generations?
How can you ensure that tomorrow's poor are cared for?
How can you do your part to make sure our community continues to thrive for decades to come?

The St. Mary's Legacy Society can help you do all of this, and more …

An Invitation to Leave Your Own Legacy

We don't know what the future will bring, but we do know that compassionate health care will remain critical to the health and well-being of our community. Already, many dear friends of St. Mary's and the Tri-State have made plans to support the hospital's future through bequests and other future gifts. These expressions of trust, confidence and faith in St. Mary's and its mission mirror those of the four Pallottine Missionary Sisters who, long ago and far from home, acted on a dream that still serves us today.

We invite you to join us in continuing the tradition of the Sisters, to heal your community and thus to do your part to heal the world. As you consider leaving your own legacy, we would be honored to visit with you and discuss your plans.

The only certainty is change, but through it all St. Mary's Medical Center will remain, in the words of a morning prayer, a place "of healing, of hospitality and of hope." St. Mary's will remain, thanks to our many generous supporters and friends.

The National Leave A Legacy™ Movement

Even if you're not acquainted with bequests and planned giving, you may have heard of the Leave A Legacy™ program.

Leave A Legacy™ is a national effort to inspire people from all walks of life and all income levels to think beyond their lifespan when doing good works.

The program began as a grassroots effort in our hometown of Columbus, Ohio in 1994. One of our colleagues (and Melanie's first professional mentor) Diana Newman, CFRE, was a co-founder of this incredible effort along with Nancy Herrold Strapp.

At the time, Diana was Vice President for Advancement at the Columbus Foundation and noticed that there were few – if any – bequest gifts left to local nonprofit organizations. Curious, she pulled together a group of volunteers to ask why they thought this was. Was it a taboo subject? Were individuals unaware of the good work local organizations do? According to the group, the simple reason was this: <u>no one knew it was an option</u>.

Diana and Nancy gathered nonprofit organizations, firms of allied professionals, and community leaders to jointly encourage donors to Leave a Legacy™ to the causes and charitable organizations important to them. By adopting one clear message and marketing it widely, all kinds of nonprofit organizations are attracting bequests and other deferred gifts.

Today, Leave A Legacy™ programs are operating in 165 communities in the United States, and 24 in Canada under the auspices of the National Committee on Planned Giving (NCPG) based in Indianapolis.

There may well be a chapter in your town or city (find out at www.leavealegacy.com).

Additional Resources

Ashton, Debra. *The Complete Guide to Planned Giving.* Rev. Third Ed. (Ashton Associates, 2004)

"The Journal of Gift Planning." (The National Committee on Planned Giving) www.ncpg.org for subscription information.

Miree, Kathryn W., J.D. *Building a Planned Giving Program, Book Three: Marketing Planned Gifts: Reaching Your Donors.* (Kathryn W. Miree & Associates, Inc., 2000)

National Committee on Planned Giving, The. 233 McCrea St., Suite 400, Indianapolis, IN 46225, www.ncpg.org.

Panas, Jerold. *Asking: A 59-Minute Guide to Everything Board Members, Volunteers, and Staff Must Know to Secure the Gift.* (Emerson & Church, Publishers, 2002, www.emersonandchurch.com)

Panas, Jerold. *Mega Gifts: Who Gives Them, Who Gets Them,* Second Edition. (Emerson & Church, Publishers, 2005, www.emersonandchurch.com)

"Planned Giving Today: The Practical Newsletter for Gift-Planning Professionals." PGToday.com for subscription information.

The Stelter Company. 10435 New York Avenue, Des Moines, IA 50322. 800-331-6881, www.stelter.com

THANK YOU

If we've learned anything through the process of writing our first book, it's that we'd have little to say without the countless donors, volunteers, colleagues, professional advisors, and valued loved ones who have shared our respective journeys. We value their insights, are inspired by their selflessness, and learn from them every day.

While listing all of them would be absolutely unwieldy, we extend our sincerest thanks to the following:

Sam, Catherine, Lovetta, Theresa, Jean, Lorraine, Osceola, Mike & Colleen and the many other gracious and generous donors whose lives inspire us daily.

The countless volunteers and development professionals whose dedication to their organizations is truly amazing.

To the religious leaders of the Franciscan Sisters of the Poor, Cabrini Mission Foundation, the Sisters of Bon Secours, and the Pallottine Missionary Sisters who understand and realize the significance and value of legacy giving.

So many of our colleagues who shared their experiences with us including Tom Bankston, Wayne Burton, Richard Friedman, Christine Maraia, Kim Munafo, Diana Newman, Garth Potts, David Sheils, Michael Stautberg, and Pat Ward.

The memory of Jim Potter, charitable gift annuity mentor and guru.

Susan Carey Dempsey and Michael Hoffman of Changing Our World, Inc. who thought of us when the publisher asked them for author suggestions.

Dawn Hensley and Tim Nawn of David Valinsky Associates for their editing, computer skills, willingness to read (and re-read) countless drafts, and general good natures.

John Danaher, Kathy Muskopf, Joann Seaman; Sr. Lucille Souza,

MSC; Sr. Bernadette Anello MSC; and Sandy Turner for permission to reprint their organizations' materials.

Steve Abbott and Michael Roediger for their invaluable input as our first readers/guinea pigs.

David Dachner for his legal advice.

And last, but certainly not least, Jerry Cianciolo, for his candor, editing expertise, and zealous commitment to clarity and good humor as he gently led two novices through the process of writing their first book

ABOUT THE AUTHORS

DAVID VALINSKY

David has enjoyed a varied career in the nonprofit world, spanning more than 25 years in executive positions with Jewish Community Centers, hospitals and health systems. One of his most meaningful experiences was serving as an adjunct consultant for US AID in Croatia on behalf of the Franciscan Sisters of the Poor Foundation. Development, marketing, relationship building and creativity have always been primary elements of these experiences.

Since forming David Valinsky Associates (DVA) in 1998 (www.davidvalinsky.com), he and his team have continued to work with hospitals, social service agencies, religious groups, legal foundations and arts organizations on capital and endowments campaigns, planned giving, and strategic development planning.

David has degrees from the University of Pittsburgh and the University of Wisconsin-Milwaukee and has earned the Chartered Advisor in Philanthropy© (CAP©) professional designation from the American College.

He and his wife, Lorrie Rosenberg Valinsky, an audiologist, live in Bexley, Ohio. They have one daughter, Alexandra, who is currently a student at Northwestern University. David can be reached at www.davidvalinksy.com.

MELANIE BOYD

Melanie shares the same circuitous route to her chosen field shared by many of her colleagues. Following eight years as a college instructor of composition, public speaking, and literature, she took her first development position at a community corrections agency.

After many years in the profession, she still wakes up with a smile, secure in the knowledge that she'll face a variety of challenges and opportunities working alongside dedicated development professionals, tireless volunteers, and incredible donors.

Melanie holds degrees from Ohio University and the The Ohio State University. She currently lives in Columbus, Ohio with Farley, the best dog in the world.

The Gold Standard
In Books for Nonprofit Boards

Each can be read in an hour • Quantity discounts up to 50 percent

Fund Raising Realities Every Board Member Must Face
David Lansdowne, 112 pp., $24.95.

If every board member of every nonprofit organization in America read this book, it's no exaggeration to say that millions upon millions of additional dollars would be raised.

How could it be otherwise when, after spending just *one* hour with this gem, board members everywhere would understand virtually everything they need to know about raising major gifts. Not more, not less. Just exactly what they need to do to be successful.

In his book, *Fund Raising Realities Every Board Member Must Face: A 1-Hour Crash Course on Raising Major Gifts for Nonprofit Organizations*, David Lansdowne has distilled the essence of major gifts fund raising, put it in the context of 47 "realities," and delivered it in unfailingly clear prose.

Nothing about this book will intimidate board members. It is brief, concise, easy to read, and free of all jargon. Further, it is a work that motivates, showing as it does just how doable raising big money is.

Asking
Jerold Panas, 112 pp., $24.95.

It ranks right up there with public speaking. Nearly all of us fear it. And yet it is critical to our success. Asking for money. It makes even the stouthearted quiver.

But now comes a book, *Asking: A 59-Minute Guide to Everything Board Members, Staff and Volunteers Must Know to Secure the Gift*. And short of a medical elixir, it's the next best thing for emboldening you, your board members and volunteers to ask with skill, finesse … and powerful results.

Jerold Panas, who as a staff person, board member and volunteer has secured gifts ranging from $50 to $50 million, understands the art of asking perhaps better than anyone in America. He knows what makes donors tick, he's intimately familiar with the anxieties of board members, and he fully understands the frustrations and demands of staff.

He has harnessed all of this knowledge and experience and produced a landmark book. What *Asking* convincingly shows — and one reason staff will applaud the book and board members will devour it — is that it doesn't take stellar communication skills to be an effective asker.

Nearly everyone, regardless of their persuasive ability, can become an effective fundraiser if they follow a few step-by-step guidelines.

Emerson & Church, Publishers

The Gold Standard in Books for Nonprofit Boards

The Fundraising Habits of Supremely Successful Boards
Jerold Panas, 108 pp., $24.95

Over the course of a storied career, Jerold Panas has worked with literally thousands of boards, from those governing the toniest of prep schools to those spearheading the local Y. He has counseled floundering groups; he has been the wind beneath the wings of boards whose organizations have soared.

In fact, it's a safe bet that Panas has observed more boards at work than perhaps anyone in America, all the while helping them to surpass their campaign goals of $100,000 to $100 million.

Funnel every ounce of that experience and wisdom into a single book and what you end up with is *The Fundraising Habits of Supremely Successful Boards*, the brilliant culmination of what Panas has learned firsthand about boards who excel at the task of resource development.

Fundraising Habits offers a panoply of habits any board would be wise to cultivate. Some are specific, with measurable outcomes. Others are more intangible, with Panas seeking to impart an attitude of success.

In all, there are 25 habits and each is explored in two- and three-page chapters … all of them animated by real-life stories only this grandmaster of philanthropy can tell.

Fund Raising Mistakes that Bedevil All Boards (& Staff Too)
Kay Sprinkel Grace, 112 pp., $24.95

Fundraising mistakes are a thing of the past. Or, rather, there's no excuse for making one anymore. If you blunder from now on, it's simply evidence you haven't read Kay Grace's book, in which she exposes *all* of the costly errors that thwart us time and again.

Some, like the following, may be second nature to you:

• "Tax deductibility is a powerful incentive." It isn't, as you perhaps know.

• "People will give just because yours is a good cause." They won't.

• "Wealth is mostly what determines a person's willingness to give." Not really. Other factors are equally important.

Other mistakes aren't as readily apparent. For example: "You need a powerful board to have a successful campaign." Truth be told, many are convinced that without an influential board they can't succeed. Grace shows otherwise.

Then, too, there are more nuanced mistakes:

• "We can't raise big money - we don't know any rich people." Don't believe it. You can raise substantial dollars.

• "Without a stable of annual donors, you can't have a successful capital campaign." In fact you can, but your tactics will be different.

• "You need a feasibility study before launching a capital campaign." Turns out, you might not.

Emerson & Church, Publishers

The Gold Standard in Books for Nonprofit Boards

Big Gifts for Small Groups
Andy Robinson, 112 pp., $24.95

If yours is among the tens of thousands of organizations for whom six- and seven-figure gifts are unattainable, then Andy Robinson's book, *Big Gifts for Small Groups*, is just the ticket for you and your board.

Robinson is the straightest of shooters and there literally isn't one piece of advice in this book that's glib or inauthentic. As a result of Robinson's 'no bull' style, board members will instantly take to the book, confident the author isn't slinging easy bromides.

They'll learn everything they need to know from this one-hour read: how to get ready for the campaign, who to approach, where to find them; where to conduct the meeting, what to bring with you, how to ask, how to make it easy for the donor to give, what to do once you have the commitment – even how to convey your thanks in a memorable way.

Believing that other books already focus on higher sum gifts, the author wisely targets a range that's been neglected: $500 to $5,000.

Robinson has a penchant for good writing and for using precisely the right example or anecdote to illustrate his point. But more importantly he lets his no-nonsense personality shine through. The result being that by the end of the book, board members just may turn to one another and say, "Hey, we can do this" – and actually mean it.

How Are We Doing?
Gayle Gifford, 120 pp., $24.95

Ah, simplicity.

That's not a word usually voiced in the same breath as 'board evaluation.'

Or brevity … and clarity … and cogency.

Yet all four aptly describe Gayle Gifford's book, *How Are We Doing: A 1-Hour Guide to Evaluating Your Performance as a Nonprofit Board*.

Until now, almost all books dealing with board evaluation have had an air of unreality about them. The perplexing graphs, the matrix boxes, the overlong questionnaires. It took only a thumbing through to render a judgment: "My board's going to use this? Get real!"

Enter Gayle Gifford. She has pioneered an elegantly simple and enjoyable way for boards to evaluate *and* improve their overall performance. It all comes down to answering some straightforward questions.

It doesn't matter whether the setting is formal or casual, whether you have 75 board members or seven, or whether yours is an established institution or a grassroots start-up. All that matters is that the questions are answered candidly and the responses openly discussed.

Emerson & Church, Publishers

The Gold Standard in Books for Nonprofit Boards

Great Boards for Small Groups
Andy Robinson, 112 pp., $24.95

Yours is a good board, but you want it to be better.
- You want clearly defined objectives …
- Meetings with more focus …
- Broader participation in fundraising …
- And more follow-through between meetings

You want these and a dozen other tangibles and intangibles that will propel your board from good to great. Say hello to your guide, Andy Robinson, who has a real knack for offering "forehead-slapping" solutions – "Of course! Why haven't we been doing this?"

Take what he calls the "Fundraising Menu." Here, board members are asked to generate a list of all the ways (direct and indirect) they could assist in fundraising. The list is prioritized and then used to help each trustee prepare a personalized fundraising agreement meeting his specific needs.

Simple, right? Yet the Fundraising Menu is the closest thing you'll find to guaranteeing a board's commitment to raising money.

Great Boards for Small Groups contains 31 brief chapters. In fact the whole book can be read in an hour. Funny thing, its impact on those who heed its advice will last for years.

The Ultimate Board Member's Book
Kay Sprinkel Grace, 114 pp., $24.95

Here is a book for *all* of your board members:
- Those needing an orientation to the unique responsibilities of a nonprofit board,
- Those wishing to clarify exactly what their individual role is,
- Those hoping to fulfill their charge with maximum effectiveness.

Kay Sprinkel Grace's perceptive work will take board members just one hour to read, and yet they'll come away from *The Ultimate Board Member's Book* with a firm command of just what they need to do to help your organization succeed.

It's all here in 114 tightly organized and jargon-free pages: how boards work, what the job entails, the time commitment involved, the role of staff, serving on committees and task forces, fundraising responsibilities, conflicts of interest, group decision-making, effective recruiting, de-enlisting board members, board self-evaluation, and more.

In sum, everything a board member needs to know to serve knowledgeably is here.

Emerson & Church, Publishers